a writer who shares too much
could also be called a poet.

Contents

Interlude

a disclaimer:

sometimes i don't know how to write
the words don't seem to fit
they seem to kind of kick and fight
and often test my wit

writing doesn't need to be good
good is categorisation
just throw them onto the page however
and overcome stagnation.

mental blocks i brush aside
and call it 'being focused'
but mental blocks should help me decide
when i need to write the most...est?

dissonance

[dɪsənəns]
a lack of harmony; discord

A moment of stillness…

Burnt out wisdom lingering

as I search for something to do.

The pile increases

with the tension in my head.

Failed attempts to slice

the clearest fog.

Seeing everything

except what's hidden, I wonder –

what am I missing?

What happens around me

that I am too scared to see?

Conflict.

Calm.

Collection

    Two truths and one lie?

Fake it till you make it, I guess.

    A cliff edge

descending into blind fantasy.

Endless and inescapable.

    It's funny how you find your niche.

Niche? Wannabe?

    Kinda funny

everyone's niche is an imitation.

Guess you have to be fake

    to find out what's real.

I try to find peace
and all I find is traffic.

I try to hear the rustling leaves
and all I hear is traffic.
I try to smell the sweetened earth
and all I smell is traffic.

I try to taste the autumn breeze
and all I taste is traffic.
I try to touch a dusty path
and all I feel is traffic.

I try to find peace
and all I find is traffic.

An ignorant woman's Guide to Bliss:

I envy the birds
although the birds have trouble enough.
They're too busy surviving to worry about love –
falling in, falling out
forgetting it's a part of life.
Life will come in phases.
Outgrowing people
and
inevitably
outgrowing love.

Searching for people to care for,

so focused on our flaws

that we don't realise

someone thinks we've got our heads screwed on.

We'll all look after someone—

others or otherwise.

sat in my room on a sunny afternoon -
another butt among many.
clouds in my mind, and i was blinded
and i was alone again.

watching leaves fall, we huddled in the hall
passing one between us.
another to reflect - alexa, play cigarettes after sex.
and i was alone again.

scrolling down instagram, i heard the door slam.

the afternoon babble ceased.

the handle turned as the sunset burned

and i was alone again.

melancholy forming as i woke up late morning,

to smooth jazz and a brew.

i had got through talking to people barely walking

and i was alone again.

The wind
threatening to carry me away.
Pulling me to and fro,
from one thing to the next.
A beeline
with no pit stops.

you appreciated me when i wasn't myself
but i appreciate you for that.
you provided me with security
and i tossed you aside.
i wonder what you'd think
if you saw me now...

maybe our hands would have grown
to fit perfectly together.
maybe our fingers would intertwine
in a way i never let us try.
maybe our hearts would pump
more blood through our veins
until our pulses fell into a beat
and we became one.

would you still see what you saw then?

in a way, i hope,

in a way, i hope not.

would i still see in you what i saw then?

would there be new pieces to you?

would you be chipped by experiences

in the time we have been apart,

the small indents building new stories

you could tell me?

10:51am

Salt-stained steps.

Sitting in the stairwell—cold and quiet

Far away from the rest of life.

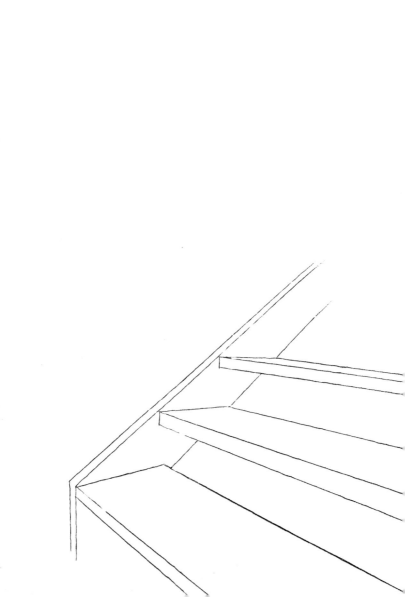

My brain walks in circles.

It runs the marathon from finish to start,
beating the record, but disqualified
before I had even begun.

I saw the arrows and thought—fuck it
I know better than them.
I'm doing it my way.

Waiting on the countdown
like Guy Fawkes
1, 2, 3. 3, 2, 1.

Unclear instructions
and a wandering mind.
No way out and too many ways in.

So much to think about
that my brain stands in limbo,
shifting from foot to foot.

i
am half asleep
my eyes don't want to make a peep

under the lid
of a tired kid
the eye sees illusions

i think of the hours ahead
how soon I can come home to bed
and pretend I've not a care in the world

These colours set me off on a roll.
I can't read anything else.
time is going so unbelievably fast and
my pen can't keep up with my
mind.

Writing keeps me sane?

I tried to make time speed up, but it
created to much time for my mind to think
and create a worse mess.

21

Sober thoughts = bad
Trying
    trying to keep up my mind
won't make words
    everything is still moving around
me
and   I've forgotten how to write

I can't look at myself in the
mirror or my ribs are bigger than
my hips —
            my arms are silver
fish who can't spell names.
                    for real tho
                    ZX

Stolen stimulation.

Plushies abandoned for pleasure,

Curiosity of a kid,

consequent woman

in one body.

Staying in or staying out?

They never stay consistent.

A narcissistic demeanour,

as soon as the door shuts, one-eighties

into a hidden self,

and the conflict hits again.

Staying in or staying out?

It's a cold, winter's night.
Not cold enough to snow,
but a heavy drizzle.
Enough to dampen spirits.

Somewhere, if I looked hard enough,
I could probably spot a star or two,
but the sky is drowsy
and the air is still, heavy,
pressing me to the ground.

The bluebird chirps.

And chirps.

And chirps.

And chirps.

And chirps.

And thunder rolls, shaking the atmosphere.

She sits in the cherry tree

It's branches slowly wilting.

Slowly

going to ruin.

Fruity haze

Like a morning mist

Like lustrous coffee

Even the sun's got a blanket on

A quilted coat of silver

Waking up softly

Lusty Glaze

A dream in a head

Keen to explore

She could be gone

In truth or illusion

Before she gets bored

Do you ever look at someone and think
'You should be older than me,
but your flamboyant footsteps say otherwise
and your blunt blade of a tongue,
once sharp—maybe dulled
from being pushed to the ground
time after time,
that blade slices
right through the middle of my patience.'

a crystalline lake glides through the valley

carving into cracks we do not see.

caressing the cold, bare skin of Gaea,

a loving hand - calm and free.

I walk the path of life

and I will find inner peace.

she cries just a little more each moment.
salty rivulets trickle over the sides
of sleepy crags, their sharpness soothed
by the silver-tongued, ever-growing tides.

falling from herself, she senses danger.
fearful of a wind so faint.
she shrinks beneath Sun's majesty -
the fragility of freedom without constraint.

I walk the path of life.

Sometimes it's dirt,

sometimes concrete,

Sometimes

it is deep, majestic, soul-crushing waters,

each meander startlingly tempting.

As each step reveals ground,

each day reveals new trials.

New lessons.

I walk the path of life
and I will find inner peace.

Act II

[so to speak]

Pull back the curtain and let the light in.

Let that plastic sunshine warm my skin.

Let it blind me

so all I see

is where I am meant to be.

Gather, friends, together.

Let's choose a spot.

Let's choose to shine in spots forgotten.

Dull corners like geodes of story,

overlooked in their tragic glory.

Sleepy.

Overcast in solace.

Exposed, if not for my SPF.

My solace protection factor.

A day returns

to the comfort

of my own bed.

Drowning in solace.

What better way to drown?

And yet

drowning is still drowning.

Suffocated

in content.

Picking at anything

for a fleeting thrill.

Progress rebounds to the safety

of familiarity

Prectiable.

Utterly unchanging.

Until it changes.

a solitary being stands on constant watch,

it's branches firm –

cradling the magpies as they nest in solace,

caressing the warm post-noon air,

stretching limbs across the green.

spreading safety.

The gentlest call in the morning
beckons me to the window.
Almost a melody,
encouraging me to sit and listen to Earth.

Hear her vibrations,

entwined imperfectly into ragged breaths,

city hums, rustling leaves.

Feel how our lives move with her, because of her.

Conversations flow,

words destroy,

flocks relocate.

She understands us

more than we understand ourselves.

She made us.

She watches as three, two, one,

And our attention has moved on.

A moving picture book
of people living lives.
Rising in the bedroom,
Sinking in the lounge.
Cooking in the kitchen,
smoking in the kitchen.

Windows cracked open,
releasing sounds
of joy,
of laughter -
of anything and everything.

Blank squares waiting
to spring into life
at the flick of a switch.
A new face,
a new mood.
A new day.

5:24am

the clouds are so dappled

they could be sky and the sky black holes,

were it not for the stars, so obviously twinkling,

appearing to move

like distant planes through Zeus' realm.

i hear the resting sounds of the city

charging up for the day.

the air is clean, cool and crisp.
i relish a slow inhale.
rubber-tinged air travels into my nose,
through my head.
the birdsong into my ears,
creating the soundtrack
of their morning school run.

there are main lights, fairy lights,

lights forgotten,

lights turned on

to guide a neighbour through their draughty kitchen

and the city lights.

i could walk through the city in this moment

and almost feel safe.

my body feels grounded,
having woken up hot and sober
after falling into sleep.
a chance to breath,
be present.
do nothing but
be.

lying in my bed, still warm from dreamless sleep,
i can breathe deeper than i remembered i could.

is this the beginning of another level?
not one singular moment,
but thousands of moments
so small
and challenges
so informal
that one day you realise you've changed.

the city reluctantly wakes up.
everything seems to drag slightly.
the car engines sound,
working extra hard
to make that morning work run.
an early bird opens the courtyard bin
and throws his worries in there,
leaving room
to pick up new ones today.

Usually, the air is still.

Nothing but a faint beep

like something is about to blow.

Your phone's dead, so you have no clue

if the last train will even show up.

You question

whether your jacket is big enough to use as a blanket

and how you might sleep across the chairs

without the armrests sticking into your spine

But today, the air hums with chatter.

Strangers offer tea from a flask

and wax lyrical about how shit the city was.

The lights from the tree ripple in the corner of your eye.

You have time to spare, knowing

that barely 40 minutes away is a meal

and warm settees and a TV

and a place you can be comfortable.

A stream of blue and burgundy
kids hold me back on the platform,
all of us ready to get home.
I'm stuck in the divide, holding my uke in my arms
as people push past me without a second thought,
all of us ready to get home.
I'm unwilling to press play,
content to bask in background noise,
ready to get home.

A concealed purpose.

You don't expect to find it

but you feel content.

Content to know that 'best' doesn't exist

and with contentment comes gratitude.

Finding interest and meaning

in the uninteresting and meaningless.

Motivation dares to venture

so even time out becomes time in.

Content

with the productive string of torment in your head –

just enough to keep moving.

Salad leaves and chickpeas

Simple and effective.
You don't know till you've tried.
Little gems hidden in a mass
of things that aren't so refreshing.
Give them a chance and they'll pull through.

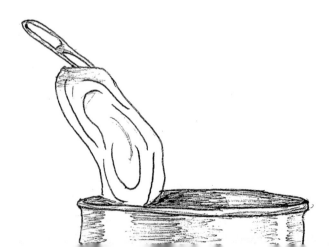

Gentle and reliable

but they won't wait forever.

Don't leave it too late.

Give them a shot.

Give the underdogs a chance to shine.

Why do we need a mask?

Why,

in freeing feelings conserved,

does our support system go black?

We aren't let down gently

with a sympathetic word.

As we beg to unpack

building baggage

we are left unheard.

Projections,

reflections,

beast

and burden.

Moulded clay crushed -

lying, uncertain.

Clinging to the hope

of truth in the design -

breaking the bond

that couldn't stand time.

something like a wrench twisting in ur chest.

loose.

sunken.

unwavering like an ice cube down ur back

that you can't catch.

see.

stop.

a drop of rain predicts a storm.

painful winds gripping you,

dragging you down

to the depths

of

Hell.

soothing kisses from the mother of all
as you fall.
the ground supporting your head
as your breathing slows.

There is wisdom there. I can see it.

It's veiled in something I don't understand.

The way baby monkeys learn to talk.

How they mimic their mother, picking berries off trees.

It is fine, fine cloth.

Each string is a word,

a look,

a breeze in the air that collided with your mind

and your anger increased tenfold.

What's on the other side?

Is it a child,,

tangled in his woven sheets

after too many nightmares?

Or do his matured hands pull it around himself,

waiting for someone

to hold them, take them

and he can finally reveal himself,

unafraid to be shunned

or spat at

or loved unconditionally?

Different lives.

Different dimensions.

Finishing at five,

waking at seven.

Paths in the kitchen

casually coincide.

'Good morning', 'Good night'

through a door closed behind.

I'm having breakfast,

you're having supper.

The daily intersection

with your Maccies and my cuppa.

She spread out across the green

Welcoming Sun's rays and inviting them to warm her skin.

Pleasures of the city are all well and good.

She is not ashamed to say

She appreciates the clumsy human world

She thrives in the city and the city thrives in her.

People surround her as she surrounds people.

Her 5am returns home defeat time

and yet

her being is natural.

Her spirit lives in a vessel prepared to take on the world.

Ice cream candle

Burning bright and colourful,
pulled as the climates take a gentle hold,
one moment smooth and warm and comfortable,
the next hard and bold.
Sticking to your soul comfortably
Like it's been there all along.
Cool, but impatient
like the early bird's song.

It's coming.
That moment.
the Fates' watched component.

@phoenix.greaves

Printed in Great Britain
by Amazon

28892333R00057